Comprehensive Guide On How To Attract A Man And Winning Back Your Ex

By

Ewache Mary Ene

Table of Contents

Chapter One

It’s easy to attract a guy and make him like you. The hard part is knowing how to make a guy fall in love with you.

You don’t have to change yourself or pretend to be dumb just to make a man you like feel comfortable around you. If you want to make a man fall in love with you, you need to understand men and their ways and use them to your advantage.

Let’s be honest, men are simple creatures.

While they hardly ever divulge their feelings or give you an insight into what they’re thinking, they actually are very simple and don’t need or want too much from anyone.

When it comes to love, however, almost all men are fairly similar.

You may make grand gestures to a guy and expect that he'll fall in love with you for those reasons, but those may not be the reasons at all. When learning how to make a guy fall in love with you, it all comes down to knowing how a guy thinks.

How to tell if he's already in love with you
Before you try to make him fall in love with you, do you know if he loves you already? Some guys are head over heels for a girl and the girl probably doesn't have a clue. And this is because guys aren't forthcoming with their feelings!

They like to hold onto them a bit too tight. But there are still some ways he shows you he loves you.
Is he talking about the future with you? Does he consider your opinion when it comes to his job, where he'll live in the future, or even

how to react to certain news? If so, he likes you already!
You can also tell how he feels about you when you're sick. We know this sounds odd, but pay attention to how he treats you or tries to stay in touch when you're feeling ill or upset.

Does he reach out or take care of you and make sure you're comfortable or just give minimal effort?
Now there are two things you need to pay attention to when it comes to winning a guy's heart.

1. You need to understand the reasons that make a girl attractive in a guy's eyes, and what makes a guy fall in love. And secondly,

2. You need to learn HOW to make a guy fall in love with you, and choose you over anyone else in the whole world.

So let's take this one step at a time, and talk about the reasons guys fall in love first, before reading the ways to hook him hard in love.

The secret reasons guys fall in love with a girl

Before you learn a few handy tips on how to make a guy fall in love with you, you need an insight into the male mind. According to many surveyed guys, these are the little things that make a man fall in love with you.

1. Your attitude – or lack thereof

When a girl is attitude-free most of the time and just goes with the flow, a man will fall in love with her very easily. It puts him at ease when he doesn't have to worry about getting an attitude from you about something trivial.

2. Your kindness

A woman who can put others before herself is a huge turn-on for a man. He realizes that she can care for not only herself but also for him and anyone else that comes into their lives.

3. How open you are
Open to trying new things and just open-minded in general. Guys can fall in love with any girl who allows them to be themselves without judging and just being open to the ideas they formulate— no matter how silly they are.

4. The way you smell
No. Not how you smell after dousing yourself in “old lady” perfume. He falls in love with the way you smell in the morning or freshly out of the shower. The real you.

5. How well do you get along with his family

And by family, we mean his mother. If you can get along with a man's mother, that is just another reason he's going to fall in love with you!

6. The way you treat his friends
You should indeed treat your man's friends like you treat him—minus the sex stuff, of course. If you treat his friends like you care about them, it will only make him fall in love with you more.

7. How you always want to know how his day went
He might roll his eyes and pretend like he's annoyed with you always asking about his day but, truth be told, he loves it and it will make him fall in love with you.

8. Because you "get him"
If he's having a bad day and doesn't even have to tell you that he's crabby or upset but

you understand anyways and give him his space, it'll contribute to him falling in love with you.

If you just get the way he is and he doesn't have to talk too much about it, he's going to fall a little bit more in love every day.

9. The way you always want to look cute for him

It's not the fact that you DO look good that makes a man fall in love with you. It's the way that you always want to look good for him.

He appreciates the way you want to look good just to make him happy.

10. Your adorable attempts at cheering him up

Even though he might shoo you away when he's in a grumpy mood, your cute little goofy faces and attempts at cheering him up do wonders when it comes to making him fall in love with you.

11. How you always steal his clothes
Again, he might pretend he's frustrated that you always snag his favorite hoodie, but he loves the way it looks on you and that you want to be surrounded by him all the time.

12. You laugh at his jokes, even if they're not funny
And he knows they're not funny but he just wants to see you laugh. Knowing you will laugh no matter what is a definite reason why he falls in love with you. [Read: 35 tempting ways to make a guy want you and dream of being with you]

13. How you look in the morning
He couldn't care less about you getting all dolled up on the weekends. What makes a

man fall in love with you is the sleepy way you roll over and groan in the morning and how your hair is messed up and you're fresh-faced.

14. The amount of emojis you use to express one emotion

Your man might not be about using emojis himself, but he sure loves that you have to send him eight emojis just to say good morning. It's such a little thing, but it makes him fall even harder for you.

15. How you snuggle up to him in the morning

When you're just waking up but not ready to commit to the daytime quite yet and you drape yourself over him and snuggle into his side, it makes him fall way more in love with you.

16. How you don't judge

A girl who thinks of everyone as equal and doesn't judge people will always make a guy fall harder in love with her. He likes to know you won't judge him for the little things he does and that you keep an open mind about everything.

17. How you try to cook for him, even if it's an epic fail. Even if you fail and end up making a burnt casserole, he loves that you wanted to make something special for him.

How to make a guy fall in love with you
Now you know what a guy looks for, it's time to get practical. Use these tips and you'll see how easy it can be to connect with a man and make him desire you.

And what's the best part? Well, you don't need to change a thing about yourself!

1. Dress attractively

Men are visual, and women know this better than anything else.

When you're out with the man you like, dress your best. If you see him grinning widely or taking discreet glances at your attire, you know you've hit the nail.

But dressing attractively doesn't just stop working its magic there. If he sees other men staring at you or admiring you, it'll only make him desire you more. Men are extremely competitive when it comes to wooing women.

Win the attention of other men in the room, and the man you like will do anything to get more attention from you. And of course, he'll realize how lucky he is to be with you.

2. Be pleasant and smile often

Men can't ever resist a cute smile. And if you can be pleasant and warm when you're with him, he'll love you for it.

If you want to know how to make a guy fall in love with you, tuck your hair behind your ear as you answer an awkward question, act a bit coy when you're being complimentary, and laugh at his jokes even if you've heard it before.

If a guy is attracted to you, he'd want to impress you with his funny, heroic tales. By reassuring him that you're having a nice flirty time, you'd make him feel better about himself. And a man always loves a woman who can make him feel like a better man!

3. Don't be rude

Men are completely put off by rude or arrogant women. If you can be rude to your date or even a waiter, he wouldn't be able to help but wonder if it's only the tip of the rude iceberg.

Men love a woman who can take a stand, but if it's in the form of arrogance, he'd stay a mile away from falling in love.

4. Connect with him intellectually

Flirty conversations are sweet and cute, and the man you like will love the fact that he's able to make you blush and go pink. But all flirting and no seriousness can get boring after a while.

On your dates together, try and connect with him intellectually now and then. Speak to him about his career goals, his ambitions, and aspirations, and let him see that he can have a meaningful life-altering conversation with you.

5. Work your eye contact

It's been seen that romantic eye contact can make two people fall in love with each other in no time. The next time you're having a conversation with him, stare deeply into his eyes as he talks to you.

You can smile or flirt, but every time your eyes meet, let the eye contact linger even if both of you aren't exchanging words. It makes the guy feel warm and fuzzy and would stir his heart. This is one of the biggest ways how to make a guy fall in love with you.

6. Lingering soft touches
If there's ever a way of knowing how to make a guy fall in love with you and be a flirty tease at the same time, this is it.

Men can't resist a lingering woman's touch. The next time you're with him, be it clasping palms, hugging each other goodbye, or just crossing the street, let your touch linger softly for a moment longer than necessary.

Your touch would be incredibly exciting for the guy you like, and you'll spark a romantic chemistry in no time.

Want to take this up a notch? Wear soft or satiny fabric when you go out on a date with the guy you like. He would have a hard time keeping his hands off you! [Read: How to flirt by touch and use subtle body language to seduce a guy]

7. Don't be easily available

This is tricky, but it's a great way to make a man fall in love with you. When you're in love with someone, you want to be with that person and spend more time with them. But when you can't be with the person you like, you end up missing the person a lot more.

Once you know the guy likes you a lot too, try to skip an occasional date now and then. While it's important to spend a lot of time together until the guy falls in love with you, it's equally important to give some space now and then to make sure he understands how special you are, and how much he needs you. [Read: How to play it cool with a guy without being too distant or clingy]

8. Show off your talents

If you want to know how to make a guy fall in love with you, learn to surprise him with your talent. He may like you for the person you are, but to completely make him fall for you, you have to let him know that you're a bundle of happy surprises, waiting to be explored.

Show off your talent and awe him with the things you do, be it at a karaoke bar or while dancing, or even while karting or playing the piano. Give him a chance to see your talent and admire you for the awesome person you are.

9. Don’t always agree with him
Compatibility is of great essence in a happy relationship. But you don’t always have to accept what the guy says or do what he wants to do. Sometimes, a minor disagreement can take him off guard, but it’ll make him respect your opinions a lot more.

Remember, a man likes to flirt with a fun girl and have a serious conversation with an intellectual girl. Give him the best of both worlds, and seriously, how can he not fall in love with you?!

10. Don’t let him know you’ve fallen for him
Men love the chase of a good romance. They take time to fall in love, but when they do, men fall hard in love. To understand how to

make a man fall in love with you, you need to know the stages of love for men.
Let the guy you like know that you like him and find him interesting, but never let him know that you've fallen head over heels for him.

Always make him wonder about how serious you are, and let him be the first one to make the move into a serious relationship. The longer the chase, the more he would want you. But at the same time, push him away too often, and he'll give up on the chase. Play hard to get, and yet, warm up to him often.

11. Laugh at his jokes
This is pretty simple. If he makes a joke, just laugh at it. This requires little effort if you think he's funny. You'll laugh naturally. The key here is to even laugh at his lame jokes.

You won't always think they're funny but just laugh anyway. It makes him feel great about himself and the better he feels around you, the more he'll actually like you. It's a little backward how it works but he'll associate you with happiness.

12. Be yourself

When it comes to understanding how to make a guy fall in love with you, it's cheesy and you've heard this a thousand times, but it's so true it needs to be said again.

The best thing you can do and the one thing that should be easier than any other tip is to just be yourself.

Let him fall in love with the real you. Enjoy life as you would without him, but just with him there. You shouldn't have to act differently or change who you are to get a guy to love you. If you do, he won't be falling for you at all, would he? Let him fall for the real you.

13. Have some confidence

If you want to know how to make a guy fall in love with you, it starts with confidence. If you don't believe in yourself, how is he going to?

You need to show him what you're made of and why you're so amazing. Believe it and you will radiate it to those around you – he included. After all, you rock!

14. Be passionate and let him see it

Passion is a very attractive quality in anyone. The difference here is that you should show him that passion.

Geek out about stuff you love. Let him see you go on a passionate rampage about your love of DIY crafting or your opinions on the education system. He'll fall for that fire inside of you.

15. Don't be afraid to show your silly side
Guys want to be able to goof off with their women. If you don't show him you can be silly and wild, it'll take him long to fall for you. So just show him that side of you right away.

Let that weird part of you out. Your friends have seen it, and so should he. Be odd and just make him laugh. He'll think it's cute and funny and THAT is how you'll win him over.

16. Admire him
And don't just do this internally. You might be thinking about how much you love that he cares so much about his health but you have to tell him those things, too. Make sure he knows how much you think about him.

Guys are very insecure when it comes to these types of things. They can't read your mind and so they don't know how you feel. Tell him and that reassurance will give him the courage to admire you back.

17. Ask him for advice

We know this seems silly and like it doesn't make much of a difference, but it truly does when it comes to making a guy fall in love with you. Most men are hardwired genetically to want to help. They like to provide and feel needed by you.

The more you make him feel that way, the more he'll want to be with you and therefore, may fall in love with you.

18. Get in good with his friends

This is the ticket to his heart. His friends are very important to him. Guys have even a deeper bond with their friends than girls do a lot of the time. So getting that seal of approval from them will help him fall for you.

He'll be more likely to allow himself to care deeply for you when his friends like you. So make an effort with them. Talk to them and joke with them so they get to know you well. Bonus points if you bring food when you see them.

19. Support his dreams, hobbies, and goals

If he's passionate about it, you should be right there cheering him on. Sometimes guys just need to know you'll be there to encourage them.

Once he realizes you're there for him and will help him achieve his goals, he'll fall for you.

20. Be sexual in a goofy way

You can be sexual in a very sexy way, too! However, being goofy and adorable while also maintaining that sexual vibe isn't something many women can do. If you can nail this and make him laugh while wanting you, he'll love you.

21. Allow yourself to be vulnerable
Just let yourself fall for him if you haven't already. Focus on building a strong, healthy bond with him. Let him see every part of you and get vulnerable with each other. This fosters love much better than other tactics.

22. Get his attention even before you talk to him
If you can get this right, you'd be able to start this with an advantage. Have you spoken to him already? If you haven't, make sure he notices you and gets interested in you even before your first hello.

23. Make him notice you when you're not around him
Okay, so if you guys have been talking already, that's okay. You may not be able to catch his eye as a stranger, but the fact that you guys are already on speaking terms makes things easy too.

You need to try to get this guy to notice you even when you're not talking to him. You can try to get more active on social media, so he sees a lot of great pics of yours every other day!

You can have fun with friends and have a real life that doesn't involve him. For more powerful ways to catch a guy's eye, use these suggestions on how to catch a guy's eye in any circumstance!

24. Leave a lasting impression on him

If you want a guy to fall in love with you, every time you talk to him or spend time around him, be interesting and fun. Let him remember you and smile long after you've walked away from him.

You don't need to be a clown, you just need to let the inner awesome you shine through confidently!

25. Make him realize just how awesome you are

What makes someone desirable in your eyes? To some, being unattainable does the trick, doesn't it? Remember that. Don't be easy, don't toe along his line, and don't fawn over him.

Even when you talk to him, don't appear overly interested or linger for way longer than necessary. Let him see you for the person you are, not as someone who's smitten by him.

26. Buy him little gifts

We're not talking about investing in a fancy watch, but buying him his favorite snack at the convenience store or picking him up a graphic tee with his favorite band on it can show him you're always thinking of him.

You don't need to buy expensive or extravagant things. Just little things that let him know he's always on your mind are surely enough to make him fall in love with you a little more every day.

27. Have mutual friends

The chances of falling in love when you have mutual friends are much higher. You trust your friends, and the friends that your friends have are usually very similar.

Also, people trust their friends. So, if your friends tell him that you're a great girl, there's a higher chance for him to initiate something with you.

28. It's all in the smile

Okay, we know that many girls are into mysterious guys who seem to be brooding all the time. However, for men, it's completely the opposite. It's even scientifically proven that smiling increases your attractiveness to the opposite sex.

That being said, don't do those phony smiles – that's not fooling anyone. Plus, you look creepy if the smile doesn't reach your eyes. This one is a pretty easy tip for how to make a guy fall in love with you.

29. Mirror him

Yeah, who would have thought that this would work? Now, this doesn't mean to mime him.

For example, you can start by walking at the same pace as him. This subconsciously shows that you two are in sync. However, as time passes, you'll see him matching his pace to yours – a great sign that he's into you.

30. Show interest in animals and children
If you want to know how to make a guy fall in love with you, this is a good place to start.

Unless you want kids relatively early, we would ease up on this though! Women who own animals are usually seen as better and more nurturing partners, seeing that they have experience taking care of something else other than themselves.

31. Get physical

This doesn't mean hooking up with him on the first date. This just means that you want to limit the amount of light between your bodies when you're sitting on a park bench.

You can tell the difference between when friends sit beside each other and when lovers sit beside each other. So, sit close to him because it'll show that you're interested and also increase the connection between the two of you.

32. Get it while it's hot

Who would have thought that getting a warm drink with the guy you like would increase the attraction between you two? Well, it does. It's called priming.

So, if you get a drink with him, get something warm – it shows that you have a warmer personality.

33. Be adventurous

Shockingly, there's a pretty high correlation between sexual arousal and anxiety.

So, our suggestion is to take him out of his comfort zone. Go to the amusement park or bungee jumping. Something that'll spark his adrenaline.

34. Make it red

You know that red is a sexy color, we all know it is. That being said, men perceive women who wear red as being sexier than those wearing another color.

We know black works for any occasion, but maybe it's time to try on something more striking. Mmmm... red... now that's how to make a guy fall in love with you.

35. Fill the void

Okay, that sounded depressing. What we mean by that is most people, when looking for partners, are looking for someone who possesses qualities that they don't have. That makes sense, right? It's all about creating a balance. So, if he's shy and you're outgoing, great! [Read: Do opposites attract or push people away?]

36. Keep some mystery
Listen, we know you want to tell him how crappy your last relationship was, but how about we save that for the third or fourth date? You can keep some things to yourself. Men find a little mystery to be alluring. You want him to be curious about getting to know more of you.

37. Let him take the lead
You don't have to let him take control all the time, but you should let him make some effort. If you're chasing him, he won't be

appreciating it. So, let him chase you. That's definitely how to make a guy fall in love with you.

38. Have a little patience

You need to have patience. Not just with him, but with life in general. If he's not responding how you'd like, be patient. That being said, if it's been a couple of months without the response you want, perhaps back off.

39. Don't be jealous

If you want him, you need to calm down with jealousy. If a girl's talking to him and you're glaring at him from across the room, well, it's not a good look for you. No guy wants a girl who's a stage 5 clinger.

We mean, would YOU want a guy like that? Exactly. If you want to know how to make a guy fall in love with you, ease off on the green-eyed monster.

40. Show that you're trustworthy

When men are looking for someone to fall in love with, they want someone they can trust. The same goes for you. So, you need to show him that you're trustworthy.

Of course, he needs to do the same. If he doesn't trust you, he'll always be hesitant about what to do with you.

41. Show him that you're independent

A guy wants a woman who looks like she doesn't need him. There's a reason why there's that saying that nice guys finish last. They're too nice and look like they need you.

Why do the cocky guys always get the attention? Because they act like they don't care. Same for you… you're an independent woman with her own life.

42. Be captivating
He has to be drawn in by you. He needs to be able to feel safe and open himself to you. Once he opens up to you, he's well on his way to falling for you.

43. Do what you know he loves
There are probably a lot of things you do that your man loves. Think about what he compliments you on or when it made him happier than you've ever seen him. Then do that!

If he loves when you surprise him with date night plans, do that. Maybe he also really likes it when you make him his favorite homemade dinner. Doing those things on occasion will help him fall more and more in love with you.

44. Keep your sense of humor

Life isn't always fun and games. However, the difficult times can be made a lot easier if you keep your sense of humor alive. Don't let it fall away just because you've been together for a while. Make sure he knows you still love to joke around and have fun.

Learning how to make a guy fall in love with you every day isn't always about adding something new to the relationship but continuing with the fun you're used to.

45. Be as understanding as you can be
There will be times in life when things go wrong. You won't always have control over everything, and you might be faced with a situation that's upsetting. Just be understanding. Know that your guy isn't perfect.

You don't want to forgive everything he does right away. But with the small stuff, just stay calm.

Make sure he knows he can come to you with anything. He can admit his mistakes, and you won't judge him. You should be his safe place. He shouldn't be scared to talk to you about something. When he knows he can count on you for this, he will fall in love with you even more.

46. Remember the important stuff
If he has a big day at work that could lead to a potential promotion, make sure to get up, send him a 'good luck message, and if you're around him, pour him a large coffee. Wish him luck and tell him you believe in him. Just trying to be on top of the important things to him will make him feel seen.

It's not much, but it's enough to show him that you think about him all the time.

47. Do something nice for him when he's having a rough day
Doing his chores when he's super stressed is such a loving, caring thing to do. It's a mutual thing. When he's having a really hard day at work or is working extra hours, do something nice for him.

Offer to buy him a coffee, and surprise him with his favorite snack. You don't need to anticipate his needs, but thinking of small ways to make his day easier will make any guy fall more in love with you and appreciate having such a great girl in his life.

48. Cuddle him in a so-called friendly way
Hugging and cuddling release feel-good hormones that remind you of how happy someone makes you. Even just a hug to say

goodbye, in that oh-so-friendly way can do the job.

Of course, you want it to be more than that but you have to take small steps! [Read: How to cuddle with a guy – The secrets to cuddling your guy most girls don't know]

49. Help him become a better man
This is so underrated that most women don't even give this a thought. But if you want to make him fall in love with you, and depend on you, you need to be his rock, his shoulder to lean on, and the voice that helps him become a better man.

Encourage him to achieve his dreams, motivate him, and be the woman who brings out the man in him. [Read: How to stroke the male ego and uncover the alpha side when he's down]

50. Take care of him
This may sound like we're telling you to be a '50s housewife, but we're not. When he isn't feeling well, rub his shoulders or bring him some tea.

Show him that you care when he is under the weather and want to help. You want to be teammates in life, so when one of you is down, the other helps to pick them up.

51. Don't get discouraged if it doesn't work out
Finally, all said and done, there's a chance that you've told him how you felt already, and he's either turned you down or told you he isn't ready for a relationship yet. We know, it hurts. But listen, this doesn't mean he doesn't feel anything for you.

That also means you shouldn't tie yourself to him. He could genuinely not be interested in you or there could be other reasons why he won't come forward with his emotions.

Whatever it is, do not lose hope in love, because whether it's with him or not, you will find love. [Read: 20 signs he doesn't want a relationship with you and just wants fun]

It's not what you say, it's what he thinks of you that matters

This is important. You can flirt up a storm, you can date him, heck, you can even throw yourself at him. But all said and done, learning how to make a guy fall in love with you is a subtle art.

He's got to appreciate you for who you are, and fall for the person that you are. Don't fake a brand new personality, or behave like someone else just to win him over.

Put yourself in his shoes, and ask yourself what would impress you if someone wants to make you fall in love with them. Everything starts from there.

These tips on how to make a guy fall in love with you can help you work your magic and make the one you like fall for you, just as long as you read the signs and make the right move.

The dating game is not always easy, and sometimes you might make mistakes. But you can learn how to play it cool with a guy to make him like you more.

how to play it cool with a guy

Dating is so complicated. It is something you look forward to as a teenager, but once you're actually in the midst of the adult dating world, it is massively overwhelming. Sure, dating is all about your feelings, but sometimes it's about knowing when to share those feelings and g how to play it cool with a guy.

Why do you struggle to play it cool with a guy

You're either insanely nervous for the first date or like someone and can't hold back your interest which can scare guys off. As someone who gives their all when it comes to a new relationship or even a new crush, the internal battle you're having is understandable.

You want this guy to know you're interested but don't want to come off too strong. You don't want him to think you're not interested, but you also don't want to scare him off by moving too quickly. Finding that balance can be a nightmare, especially when you m.

When you like someone, you want them to stick around. You want to do what you can to keep dating them. It makes sense.

The problem is, that what women want from a new guy and what men want from a new woman aren't always the same. You might think that going out of your way for him, cooking for him, or keeping in touch all day is what he wants from you when in fact, that is what you want from him.

Should you play it cool with a guy?
If you believe that honesty is the number one part of any relationship, playing it cool does sound a bit hypocritical. We get that. Playing it cool is, in fact, a way of holding back. But, holding back when necessary isn't lying or being dishonest.

Sometimes we can be too forthcoming too soon and realize that we confused excitement, infatuation, or even attraction with love.

Many girls have dated people before and thought their feelings were so strong only to look back at that time and realize that they were swept away in the excitement of a new romance more than that actual guy.

Understanding how to play it cool with a guy isn't about holding back your feelings or acting like you don't care. And it isn't about being mysterious or playing hard to get. Playing it cool with a guy is about not getting ahead of yourself. It is about taking your time and enjoying the present. [Read: How to be mysterious without being too distant]

How to play it cool with a guy the right way

Learning how to play it cool with a guy is easier said than done. Yes, we will offer tips and things you can do to make it easier, but controlling your excitement about a new romance is difficult.

When you gush to your friends about the amazing guy you started seeing, you fall into a trap. You want him to be your boyfriend yesterday. You crave the intimacy and closeness of a relationship more serious than where yours is at the moment.

Trying to hold back that excitement for the benefit of your potential future and happiness is like holding out on ice cream for your summer bikini body. You know it will pay off but can't help how you feel now.

Before you do any of the following to play it cool with a guy, remind yourself where not playing it cool has led you before. Did it lead you to pain or heartbreak? Did it stop the relationship before it started? Or did it make you clingy and unsure?

Think about the benefits of learning how to play it cool with a guy and go from there.

1. Stay busy

The best thing you can do when you're struggling to play it cool with a guy is to keep busy. You may be dying to text him or make plans, but if you already have plans with your friends you won't be so eager.

Keep yourself busy with projects, work, or even volunteering. It is easy to lose your cool when you are doing nothing but thinking about the new guy in your life.

2. Remember the rest of your life

We easily get overwhelmed when dating someone new. Everything we do revolves around this new romance.

The thing is, whether it works out or not, there is more to your life than this. Take time for your family and friends. Focus on all the other parts of your life.

3. Talk about something else
One of the things that makes us even more invested in a new romance is talking about it. Sure, it is great to give your BFF a play-by-play of your first date. But going on and on about this new guy will build him up in your mind.

You spend all of the lunch with your girlfriends talking about how much of a gentleman he was. How he is a doctor and is tall that you build him up better than you originally thought. This amplifies your feelings unrealistically.

4. Don’t rush it

When you find someone you think is a great match, you want to know it will work. You want to be in an official relationship. Then you’ll feel secure and no longer wonder what will happen. But, rushing into a relationship can put a lot of pressure on something new.

Enjoy the time you date. Instead of worrying about meeting his parents or introducing him to your friends, focus only on your actual connection.

5. Get off your phone

Being on your phone when you are trying to play it cool with a guy makes it so much harder. Before smartphones, it was easy to not talk to your new beau all day. Now you see a meme and want to send it to him. You have access to communication 24/7.

But over-texting can not only come off as clingy but can leave you with the feeling that you are more involved than you are.

Maybe you had two dates, but you text all day every day. That can make you think things are moving faster, but they aren't.

6. Build your confidence
A reason we thrive on a new romance is how it makes us feel about ourselves. Knowing this guy likes us boosts our confidence.

There is nothing wrong with that, but remember you are just as amazing and worthy with or without his interest.

7. Be honest about your intentions

Our excitement can get the best of us and prevent us from playing it cool with a guy. After a third date, you could picture him as your husband. But be realistic.

Do you want a relationship right now? Do you want to be committed? Be honest with yourself and your new guy about what you want from this experience.

8. Think about what you need

When a woman is dating someone new, she is often described as needy. A woman who wants a lot of attention or is high maintenance is not playing it cool. But, even though that behavior is described as needy it isn't really what you need.

You don't need him to say "good morning, beautiful" and "good night." You don't need to see him constantly. These things are nice, but you've been doing just fine on your own.

So think about what you need from a new relationship.

You want someone who is there for you when you need it. Someone who will support you and laugh with you. You don't need someone that buys you flowers for no reason or always tells you where they are or who they're with 24/7. [Read: How to stop being codependent and have a healthy relationship]

9. Enjoy the moment
The key reason we often don't play it cool with guys is that we are looking ahead instead of enjoying the moment. These times when you are first getting to know each other are the best parts. The butterflies and nerves are exciting.

Make the most of this time. Don't rush into something so serious.

10. Don't reach out first
At the beginning of a relationship, you should let the guy take the lead. That's how nature built humans – for men to be the leading person. Of course, women are independent and strong these days.

But men still like to "hunt" and "chase" women. They're not a lot different from the caveman days. So don't text or call him first. Let him initiate communication and dates, at least in the beginning.

11. Take your time texting him back
When you like a guy a lot, it's exciting to get a text from him. Because you are feeling giddy about it, there is the temptation to text him back within seconds. But when you do this, it shows that you are overeager.

And that is not how to play it cool with a guy *who may not be into you just yet*. So, take your time texting him back. Be more nonchalant and act like you aren't as excited as you are.

12. Tell him about the other plans you have
When you do talk to him, tell him how busy your life is. Tell him about the concerts you're going to with your friends or that you are taking a weekend trip.

When he knows that you have a lot more going on in your life, he knows you're not waiting around for him to text you or ask you out on a date.

This makes him more eager to pursue you and win a bigger piece of your time. It also makes him value any time that you spend with him.

This is how to play it cool with a guy. You see, you're not trying to manipulate him, you're only holding yourself back so you don't make yourself look needy and clingy in his eyes.

13. Don't put him on a pedestal
You might be incredibly infatuated with him and think he is the hottest man on earth. Also, you might wonder why he is interested in you because maybe you think he's out of your league.

But stop putting him on a pedestal. He's only a human being just like you and everyone else. He's not a god, so stop thinking that he is.

14. Don't overthink
Girls always overthink everything. So, if he's not texting as much as you want him to or taking too long to get back to you, stop inventing reasons in your head.

Don’t freak out too much when he isn’t acting the way you want him to. The more you overthink, the crazier you will make yourself.

15. Don’t be needy or obsessive
You might have an anxious-attachment style where you fear being abandoned or rejected. If you do, that causes needy and obsessive behaviors. But unfortunately, most guys don’t like it when girls act that way.

If you feel clingy, then keep it to yourself or share it with your friends. Never, ever show it to him, or else you will be your own worst enemy.

16. Don’t drunk text him
Watch how much you drink, because when you get tipsy or drunk, logic and reasoning slip away. Instead, the emotional side of you

takes over, and that is not a good way to play it cool with a guy.

If you are drinking with your friends, have someone hold your phone so you're not tempted to text him. You never know what you might say that you will regret.

17. Keep things playful and light. You want to talk about "us" and the future and/or define the relationship. But if you want to play it cool with a guy, keep things playful and light when you talk to him. You don't want to scare him off.

18. Take the physical relationship slowly
If you haven't had sex yet, then put the brakes on it a little bit. That doesn't mean you have to wait forever, but you don't want him to think that you're too easy.

You want him to know that you have standards and that you are assessing whether or not he meets them. If you have had sex with him already, then don't get needy and clingy because of it.

19. Give him space to miss you
Guys fall in love with a girl's absence. Yes, that sounds silly, but it's true. So, give him a lot of space.

Don't be so available to him all the time. When he doesn't see or talk to you very often, he will eventually miss you, and then he will like you more.

20. Tell him "no" sometimes
Sure, you are very eager to see him, but don't be ready at the drop of a hat to see him anytime. If he asks you to hang out, tell him "no" sometimes.

That doesn't mean you should play games with him, but if your life is busy, it will just be natural that you have other plans. It will make him want to see you more.

With a bit of perspective and practice, learn how to play it cool with a guy. Then, really relations p!

Chapter Two

You need to make them feel you are worth it. You need to increase your value.
You need to make them feel you're too busy for them because your life is wonderful and you have many people who would want to be with you.
You need to make your ex feel that you love yourself. If you love yourself, people will love you, including your ex.
Something you never thought would happen has happened: you lost a great guy…and now you're trying to figure out how to get your man back.
Maybe you ended things with him and realize now that you made a big mistake…
Or he ended things and you want him to realize that he made a big mistake…
Whatever caused the breakup, now you want to know how to get your man back.

I’m going to teach you some effective ways to do just that If You Broke Up With Him…

If you did the breaking up, realize that he will be nursing some serious hurt and that his ego may be bruised. You’ll have to prove yourself trustworthy. How can he be sure you won’t break up with him again?
The key is understanding and being able to explain why you broke up with him. Was something wrong in the relationship that you think could be fixed? Talk to him in a nonconfrontational way about what went wrong and discuss how things could be different.

It’s important to let him know that you want him back…but that you’re both better off with things being approached differently this time.

If He Broke Up With You…

Get to the root of why he did it. Did he express displeasure at some behavior of yours? Were the two of you constantly bickering about the same things over and over?

You need to be willing to make serious changes to win him back. He'll be skeptical if you immediately tell him you are willing to change but start by showing him that you're making the effort.

If There's Another Woman in the Picture…
If he left you for another woman, I want you to seriously question whether you want this guy back (especially if he cheated). Sure, he may seem more appealing because some other woman has her hooks in him, but let's look at the facts: he didn't respect you enough to stay away from temptation while he was in a relationship with you, so why

would you beg him back? How can you be sure it won't happen again?

Tips on How to Get Your Man Back

1. Step Away from the Situation to Evaluate the Relationship

You're not 20, so I'm willing to bet that your breakup wasn't just a heat-of-the-moment kind of thing. There was something wrong in the relationship, regardless of who ended things.

I know right now you're hurting, but I need you to put on your unbiased glasses for a moment and reflect on the relationship. It's easy to sweep the bad stuff under the rug and focus on the great stuff post-breakup, but you need to be honest about how the relationship went.

What were the flaws?

What did you argue about?

What behavior of his bothered you?

What behavior of yours bothered him?

If you're serious about getting back together, you need to have a realistic perspective to understand whether it's even worth salvaging the relationship and whether you're both willing to put in the hard work to make things right.

2. Give Him Time and Space To Realize How Awesome You Are

Particularly if he broke up with you, he may need some time away from you to realize what he's lost. So leave him alone. Follow the No Contact Rule. Vanish from his life.

You can't in any way force this man to see what he's given up. He has to do it on his own. Just give him time and space, and if it's meant to be, he'll start missing you.

3. Implement the No Contact Rule
no contact rule
If you want him back, start by following the No Contact Rule.

I already mentioned the No Contact Rule, but it's as much for you as for him. Whether you are supposed to get back with this guy or not, having spaced apart gives you both time to reflect on the relationship and what you want in the future, together or not.

When you're fresh out of a breakup, all your focus is on how to get your man back. You're in a reactive state of mind, not a proactive one. You're in crisis mode and unable to think about things.

In a scientific study published in the journal NeuroImage, researchers found that these two types of thinking, hyper-reactive and proactive, were evident in the brain's white matter. When subjects thought proactively, their brains showed more white matter. Those that thought reactively were more anxious and had less robust white matter.

So having time away from this guy can keep you from being overly reactive and give you perspective to help you decide whether you still want to know how to get your man back.

4. Be Willing to Compromise…Within Reason

I want to keep stressing the fact that, if you're successful in your strategy on how to get your man back, you both will need to make some changes. Things will never go back to how they were.

Whatever was broken, you'll need to fix it, and that likely means compromising on a few things. However, know your limits. You might compromise by agreeing to give him more alone time (that's what he complained about before) but put your foot down at the prospect of him hanging out with his ex-girlfriend.

5. Don't Try To Make Him Jealous

Again, you're not 20, so why take advice geared to younger women (and bad advice, at that)? It is okay for you to go out or be with friends while working on getting your ex back. However, do not purposely try to be seen with another man or say things that make him jealous. It is even okay to engage in an informal date and start seeing someone socially. You just can't do it to make him jealous.

Rather than focusing on how he sees you, put energy into how you see yourself. I guarantee you'll be happier getting out and being social than sitting on the couch bingeing Black Mirror. Find happiness without a man, and if he's around, believes me, he'll pay attention to that fact. It's a bruise to his ego to see you doing so well without him, so that may open the door to a conversation about getting back together when you're ready.

6. Work On Your Self Confidence

confident woman

Being happy, with a guy or not, starts by finding your inner confidence.

The truth is: I don't know if this guy is the right one for you. I don't know whether working on how to get your man back is the right move for you or not. But what I do know is that improving your self-confidence will help you, both in this relationship and in future ones, if there are any. Confidence will help every aspect of your life, from love to work, so don't overlook its importance!

7. Pamper Yourself: Look Your Best to Feel Your Best

Again, looking good isn't to make him jealous. It may work, sure, but my goal here is to make sure you feel your best.

I know you've had some bad days where you didn't want to leave the bed (maybe you didn't, even). And that's completely part of the breakup process. But I need you to trust me when I say that you will feel a million times better if you invest in some self-care. Put on a dress you feel great in. Get your hair colored. Whatever self-care means to you, do it, because it's essential for healing, whether you reunite with your ex or not.

8. Be Honest About What Went Wrong

If you're ready to put all the blame on him, hesitate a minute. It takes two to make a relationship right…or wrong, so don't underplay your role in what happened.

That's where spending time away from him can pay off because you have space to reflect on what happened and accept it. That's essential if there's a snowman's chance in Hell of you working things out.

9. Apologize if You Hurt Him

Genuinely saying you're sorry can go a long way to winning him back.

Once you accept your role in the breakup, it's important to be humble enough to apologize for what you did. But apologize sincerely. That means not saying, "I'm sorry for hurting you, but you hurt me first!"

If you need him to apologize, and that's the only reason you're doing it, don't bother. That's not a solid foundation for getting back together.

10. Don't Play Games

I don't even need to say anything here. Just don't play games. It's simple. You're an adult, so handle the breakup like one. That'll increase the odds of you getting back together, by the way.

11. Don't Use Social Media to Poke At Him

I know women who, after suffering a breakup, post pictures with hot guys on Facebook, hoping to make their exes jealous.

It's a childish move.

12. Talk to Him About Your Relationship

Open the door to better communication this time around.

If you are going to succeed at getting your man back, you've got to open up communication, especially if the two of you had trouble talking about your relationship in the past.

Talk about what went wrong. Encourage him to tell you at the moment if something's not right so that it won't escalate into a breakup. When you talk about problems in the present, you can find ways to solve them, but if you let them build up, they end up being bigger than they were initially.

13. Know When To Move On

I sincerely hope that your efforts at getting your man back to work and that things pan out. But know that it's not always right to get back with an ex. You have to trust your gut to understand whether it's worth pursuing or not.

If you've tried to win him back and it's just not working, realize that this is the sign that it's time for you to let this guy go and move on. He's not the one for you. Save your love and energy for the right man who will be the right fit for you.

14. Don't post negativity on social media
First, your acquaintances will unfollow you, and seeing the negativity, they won't even want to go near you or introduce new people to you. Second, new friends will all know that you're sad and don't want to know you more, or else they'll get infected with your sadness. Third, for the friends who care about you — you can just go the traditional way and meet up with them and cry your eyes out.

It's really stupid to get more attention by being negative. No one likes to give that kind of attention.

15. Don't hurt yourself

Why are you hurting yourself for someone who doesn't care? That's dumb.

Don't just get into relationships easily

I know you feel hurt and you probably feel worthless right now because you feel like your ex doesn't want you. You are eager to feel loved and hopefully 'My ex will know that I'm in another relationship and my ex will feel jealous and will beg to come back.' STOP. That's not self-love. That's called my-ex-is-still-the-center-of-my-universe. Everything you do is because you want to get your ex back. But, everything you do from now on should be focused on yourself.

It may seem like they're contradictory — To get your ex back by not trying to get him/her back.

That's exactly the point.
That's what makes us human.
You always want what you don't get.
And you always want what you think is good for you. So how can you make yourself better? You can start with appearance (new haircut, new clothes, get some muscles, eat healthier, etc) and a good attitude/be open-minded. Join meditation/yoga/learn new things. Upgrade yourself with your outer appearance and inner attitude. Be the best version of yourself.

16. Go out with friends and meet new people
So now you're Version 2.0, you need to Flaunt it to others. Get out more!
Start doing something that's been on the Backburner
You need to have the courage to do what you love. That's the most important point to love yourself.

For example, if you've always wanted to try horse-riding, start learning it. Enroll in a course.

If you want to start a business, it's time to start learning how to do that and surround yourself with people who are doing the same.

If you always wanted to go back to your high school and visit your favorite teacher, it's time to do that.

If you want to try that new restaurant and want to do a pedicure, go do it.

This is the time when you just have to care about yourself.

17. Take pictures

When you go out or have new experiences, take pictures of your new and improved appearance. When you're doing your favorite things, take a picture. You can also take pictures with your friends. Be happy. Then post on social media like Instagram or Facebook. This will help you attract new

friends too! Your ex may or may not see these photos. Who cares? You're enjoying yourself and you will attract more like-minded people. But please don't post too much. Posting once every two days is a good amount to not annoy others while showing your amazing life.
While you are doing all these, don't even try to think about your ex or what he/she would like. Do what YOU like. Be the best version of yourself.

I won't be surprised if your ex starts contacting you again in whichever way. Most of them do.

And when he/she contacts you again, just treat them like an acquaintance, never treat them like an ex. Be nice. If you don't feel that you're ready to speak to him/her, then just ignore it. If they ask to meet, don't do that because although you look all healed, I know it will still hurt when you meet again.

Don't just start the relationship again after only a few calls/contact.
After all, your value is much higher now.
Your ex is just another pursuer. Let them wait a while and take as much time as you want to evaluate the person again before you get back. You might even find someone who loves you more than your ex!
Curious why I know all of this?

I've been dumped by different people before, I can't even count.

18. Time is your friend
The first thing you need to do after you break up with him is to cut off ties with him.

This sounds extreme but the truth is that if you want him to think about you, you need to make sure he has limited access to you.

Blocking him on social media, ignoring his phone calls, and avoiding the places you know he goes are all ways to get him thinking about you on the regular, even though he can't see you.

While you might be inclined to start living your best life out online so he can see you and be thinking about you, the truth is that absence makes the heart grow fonder so if he can't get access to you, he'll be looking for you.
Watch his excellent free video here.

19. Get control of the situation
The next thing you need to do is get very clear on what you need from him and keep

that handy for when he comes crawling back to you.
You don't want to seem desperate when you finally pick up the phone, so you need to get a grip on your thoughts and feelings.
Make sure you don't see him before you can control your outbursts of crying or sobbing.
And it's okay to miss your ex, cry and sob, but not in front of him while you are trying to get him to see the error of his ways.

It's best to let him think you aren't fazed by any of this. It'll drive him crazy.

20. Don't beg
Could it be that he doesn't want a relationship with you anymore?

During the time you are taking for yourself, be sure you don't seek him out and beg for him to come back. Sounds silly, but people do it.

Don't be so needy that you can't do anything without him. That might have been part of the reason he left in the first place.

Giving yourself (and him) some space means that you don't throw yourself at him. It's just bad for everyone and you'll regret it later if he only comes back because you wouldn't stop asking him to.

That's not how you get him to realize he needs to come back, which is what you want. You don't have to ask for anything. He'll come around to the idea on his own.

21. Don't bother with him

How do you get him to come around to the idea on his own? You don't bother with him.

Cut off his contact with you on social media, and il, text, and don't answer his phone calls. It sounds extreme, and it is.

You need him to be forced to think about you without seeing you or hearing from you. That's the best kind of thinking.

This means he is wondering about you wanting to know what is going on with you.

If he can't see you, he'll want to, especially if he had it in his head that you were going to come knocking after him.

Conclusion:
Learning how to get your man back will take effort. It will be hard. You may want to give up because it means facing your flaws.

But if you believe this man is worth it, then keep on keepin' on. Hopefully, you'll find that your relationship is even stronger the second time around.

www.ingramcontent.com/pod-product-compliance
Lightning Source LLC
LaVergne TN
LVHW050332160826
845677LV00014B/3601

9798846103603